Contact the author:
edwhite0142@gmail.com | www.feelingsarestupid.com

Contact the publisher:
Unprecedented Press LLC - 229 W Main Ave, Zeeland, MI 49464
www.unprecedentedpress.com | info@unprecedentedpress.com
instagram: unprecedentedpress



ISBN-13:978-1-7321964-6-9

Ingram Printing & Distribution, 2020

First Edition

Hand-Rendered Type by Dani Miché-Whiting.

Unprecedented Press

# FEELINGS ARE

~~VALID~~ ~~REAL~~ ~~PAINFUL~~

# STUPID

~~ESSENTIAL~~ ~~FUN~~

~~GOOD~~ ~~WONDERFUL~~

ED WHITE

# table of contents

# dedication

This book is dedicated to those who believed in my writing when I didn't. To my wife Janey, without you this book would never have happened. You are my biggest encourager, and my biggest believer in my dreams. To my parents, thank you for raising me so well and helping me understand that every part of my character is important and vital to impacting those around me. Dani Miché-Whiting - without your eye this book wouldn't look as great as it does! Thank you for all your hard work in helping bring this dream to life. And to Josh and all those at Unprecedented Press; thank you for helping me to fulfil this ambition and start this journey! To all of my friends, you've all played a part in this dream becoming a reality. Thank you so much.

And finally and most importantly, this work of creativity would never have happened had I not followed the words of Jesus spoken into my life. I hope these words I have written reveal an element of Jesus that you've never experienced before.

# INTRODUCTION

Two things have defined my existence: Jesus and People. One sets a standard for a life to emulate, and the other provides you with encounters with the living God, whether you realise it or not. If we are all created in His image, doesn't that mean that everyone needs to know Jesus in order to reflect his nature? There's a thought to ponder.

People are such a valuable part of this planet. They bring adventure, excitement, disappointment, frustration, happiness. The list could (and does) go on. The point is, without people life would be incredibly dull.

What do people have to do with this book? In a way, ***everything.***

As you'll quickly learn over the following pages, a key theme of this book is human connection. I value connection with people more highly than a lot of other things.

What follows is an exploration into the twists and turns my life has taken, and the experiences that have helped to define not only my life but also my identity. My hope in sharing these thoughts is that you find a connection through the words I write. These aren't simply experiences for one person. Feelings and emotions are powerful and can help you to healthily manage yourself.

With that in mind, where better to start than ***the heart?***

*(If you cringed at that thought, please keep going... it'll be worth it — I promise.)*

# THE REAL QUESTION

Sometimes I look at people I encounter and think to myself, "I wonder what their story is? What's the narrative behind those eyes?"

In a world that's flooded with face—value interactions and a society that encourages walk—by greetings (if any at all), how many people actually stop to engage with those around them? Often we seem to be so engrossed with our own daily structure that we miss out on something that's becoming gradually less important: human interaction.

I'm a millennial: I get it. I've been brought up in a society that is more connected than any other. The internet made its debut in my childhood. We're forever going to be the generation that's at risk of having a phone permanently glued to our hand. I both love and feel aggrieved by the joys of this first world society.

It's made the world that much more accessible, especially for those who maybe don't have the ability to travel to the four corners of the earth and explore the wonders there. Nowadays, you can Google Earth your way around the planet. I have friends all over the world. Technological wonders such as FaceTime and Skype and iMessage allow me to remain a part of their lives when distance should make it difficult. Answers to every day questions are now accessible not just by pressing a button… but also words"Hey Siri."…(I do love Apple really)

The beautiful irony in this is that I still remember a time when I wasn't constantly connected. When free time as a kid didn't equate to hours spent on an Xbox or PS4, but to actually hanging out and playing football with my mates. Or Power Ranger figurines — They were 'it'; but only if you had the Red Ranger. And Pokemon CARDS (incidentally I love Pokemon Go, but it's got nothing on swapping actual cards). And collecting countless seasons of football stickers. If your childhood didn't contain the words "got, got, need!" was it really a childhood?

What I'm saying is I remember a time when human fun and excitement wasn't built on something to do with a new gadget or a new technological breakthrough. That makes me happy. What makes me sad is that we seem to have lost an element of connection in all of this, which is somewhat ironic in a world of such *connectivity.*

In losing that connection, does anyone ever ask themself "*who am I?*" The reality is that it's incredibly easy to create a world that's fake. You see it with shows like *Catfish*, where someone is caught out online for pretending to be someone they're not. In a society so entwined with one another, it's now easier than ever before to present people with whatever you want your ideal world to be.

You see, reality can become selective now. You have the power to pick and choose what people in your digital reality see as your everyday life. And if you're really good, you can make that digital reality seem like your actual reality. An image is presented that might be so far removed from the truth that nobody but you would ever realise it.

*So we have a world crying out for an answer to another question — Who are you? Who are you,* ***really?***

People are so hungry for a genuine encounter with genuine humanity. It's so clear to see, but also so simple to brush over and miss completely. I think one of the reasons I'm so passionate about this topic is because I love genuine interaction with other people; finding out how they're *actually* doing, not what their five-second disclaimer says about them. "Oh I'm fine thanks" is a reaction rather than a response. I can't fathom the idea of a world where we're all just relegated to another senseless interaction, be it digital or natural. *People are created for so much more than that.*

You see, I've realised *"who am I?"* is a daily question for everyone. I wake up every morning and wonder how the day is going to unfold, and how I can affect it whilst also batting away negativity, doubt and insecurity. I either stand firm in what Jesus says about me, or I put myself in a world of danger. Emotions are powerful. Nonetheless we have all been given the ability to not let them direct our lives.

In the Great Commission in Matthew 28, Jesus is talking to the disciples before He is about to leave them. He states "All authority in heaven and earth has been given to me." As He tells the disciples to go and make disciple the nations in the name of the Father, Son and Holy Spirit, He is not speaking from a place of powerlessness. The same authority with which Jesus ministered is possessed by every one of His followers. So, we cannot afford to be passive in our actions, especially when it comes to governing ourselves. *"All authority" either means* ***"all authority"*** *or it doesn't.* That includes taking dominion over your emotions. That might be controversial and brand new information to some of you. But trust me, *that truth will set you free.* But we'll get into that a little bit later.

Before you can figure out how to answer the world's question, you must first ask yourself "who am I?" I'm not sure there is another question in the world that holds as much weight as that. Can you think of many other words that define not just yourself, but everyone else on the face of the earth? It moulds us every day, whether we realise it or not. The constant in the back of our minds is always that soul—searching idea, wrapped in confusion and rare moments of epiphany when we get glimpses of who we were created to be. To throw in a disclaimer here, I don't think that this is a question to which we will ever fully find the answer. But then part of the beauty of this journey is hidden in the mystery of answering said question. I don't profess to possess the answer to the question of who I am, and I'm going to be figuring that out for the rest of my life. I'm okay with that.

*Alright.*
Let's move on.

# CHILD'S PLAY

The biggest reason for me writing this book is because people kept telling me I should, and I finally decided to listen. One of the key voices in my ear over the years has been that of my mother. Our parent's words can carry great weight in our lives. They can be both positive, and negative, and their impact is often more unseen than seen. I've certainly noticed this for my own life. Let me stress, before I delve into this treasure chest that I have great parents. I wouldn't be the man I am without their constant guidance and encouragement over the years. They've championed me to believe in myself and my dreams, and I like to think that I've managed to do the same for them (It's a two—way street, this family stuff).

Let me also state that I realise some of you reading this might not have had the best parent examples for your own life. I'm genuinely sorry about that. But I'm hoping that through the words you're about to read, you'll be able to connect with my story and maybe see some hope in your own situation.

*Nobody is perfect.*

I know this might come as a shock to some people, but I realised this from an early age. (That's not meant to sound depressing — it's just a dose of reality because I'm British. It's what we do.) Your own upbringing is often a reflection of what your parents experienced when they were growing up, and sometimes they're trying to redefine a healthy upbringing for their own children because theirs wasn't too brilliant. I was very fortunate as a kid to have good values, values that I was allowed to take on or do my own thing. My childhood was pretty stereotypically Christian. I was brought up in a stable and happy home, going to church every weekend and enjoying the wonders of Sunday School. I also worked my way through school being that kid who was already a foot taller than all the other kids (I'm 6'5", just to clear that up and I don't remember ever being short.) I was pretty much your average Christian kid. I was quiet, nice (what a great and descriptive word that is, truly), hones and clean cut, if you will. But I wasn't perfect. Because you can't actually ever *be* perfect. It's this unattainable characteristic and stigma that has been presented to everyone as something to reach, but that reach is always going to come up short. Honestly, my understanding of the word "perfect" when I was a kid was likely completely different to what I deem it to mean now.

You see, from my perspective, when you're a kid you're one of two things:

1. One who strives to impress people/friends/family and pull out all the stops. Some might call you a try—hard, but you're actually a loving, caring person who's just trying their hardest.

2. One who sees the rules life puts in front of you, and you stick two fingers up to them, because you're an individual. You can't be defined by anything because that's conformity, and if you're individual, you can't really conform.

And therein starts the journey towards unobtainable perfection.

These two versions of the same kid, I believe, are indicative of the environment in which you're raised. If you're raised with positive influences you are told you are great, but you're also told not to step out of line. If you do, your fate is actually worse than death — *disappointed* parents. "I'm not angry at you, just disappointed." (A little piece of me just died inside). In this case you're constantly in fear of messing up in some way, whether you realise it or not. If you are option two in that list, then it's likely you've either been the good kid who just can't take it anymore, or you've always thought that the other side of the tracks was more appealing. You've had that dangerous streak in you since day one. And danger is exciting.

There's also a third option here, but one that doesn't seem to be as prevalent in society. If you're raised in an environment that encourages you to be powerful and make choices based out of knowing that you're a great person, then count yourself lucky! Knowing that you won't be judged or condemned over bad choices, but instead challenged to grow and become a better person is a great blessing. You've received a childhood that a lot of us are trying to model for our future kids, or copy right now. If that's you, take a step back and applaud your parents more than you usually might. They've done a great job, and you should damn well be thankful for that. Why am I banging on about parents and kids? Because that's where we all come from. I'm not about to explain the birds and the bees to you, but you get my drift.

You replicate what you experience. This is especially true in the home environment. Your outer world is *always* a reflection of your inner world. I am the big kid I am because of my parent's influence on my life. They taught me to be the confident and charismatic person I am today. They invested into me from a young age. But what I only recently discovered is that my story could have been very different altogether.

## THURSDAYS

I'm fourth out of five kids. So in a way I never had to deal with middle child syndrome, or being the eldest. I was the even number in an odd bunch, which is an appropriate way to describe my family, if ever there was one.

We're split into two groups of kids: Dad was married once before he met Mum, but sadly lost his first wife to cancer at a relatively young age. In that first relationship, they had three kids, so I've got three older siblings.

There's about fifteen years between me and my older sibling, but that just adds to the fun family dynamic we have. To some, the age gap between us might seem like a big deal. To me, it's just second nature. I don't even think about it as a 'thing'. We all get on, which I understand is a rare thing between family members nowadays.

You might wonder if there are any 'evil stepmother' vibes in the family, because my mum is not some of my siblings' mother. There are not. We manage to stay a cohesive and functional family unit, through any trial and tribulation we face. And believe you — me, there have definitely been some over the years, but isn't that what bonds families? Sticking together when it all hits the fan? That, and having the ability to communicate pain in a healthy way. We'll get to that later. The reason I'm telling you all this is because there's a beautiful story of redemption behind it all.

To many, the specific day of the week that you were born isn't usually that big of a deal, unless you really like some days more than others. I was born on a Thursday — the third day (that's a *Friends* reference; I do that a lot.) Thursday, November 5th, not a particularly notable day really. November 5th is Bonfire Night in the UK, where for some reason we celebrate someone trying to blow up the Houses of Parliament with gun powder by having firework displays. So I have fireworks on my birthday every year. I came into the world with a bang *cough*. (You are welcome.)

Thursdays. They're not quite Friday, but they're far from Monday. Which is good, because nobody really likes Mondays. And if they tell you they do, they're lying. Bob Geldof even wrote a song about it. I've always made the joke that I was my Dad's 50th birthday present, because I arrived three days before his own day of birth. Which also makes figuring out how old he is pretty easy. All I have to do is add my age to fifty. What I didn't realise is that my sister was also born on a Thursday. Three years after me. But the same day.

*Why is this important?*

When Dad lost his first wife to breast cancer, it was obviously a very dark time in his life. It was incredibly tough for the whole family, but whether he knew it or not, that circumstance led to him choosing to follow Jesus, and there was a shred of hope placed into the darkness. Jesus was on the case.

***Side note:*** *whether you're aware of Him or not, Jesus is always there, in the good moments and the bad. So be aware that when you're fighting uphill through what feels like a relentless storm of opposition, Jesus is there. He's there in front of you, breaking the ground for you to move forward. He's there beside you, guiding your steps. And He's there behind you, holding you up when you feel like collapsing. He's always got your back. And He always will. Always a good reminder, that. If you can't find Jesus in the toughest situations you encounter, then where can you? If He's easier to spot in the difficult times then it makes it more obvious to spot Him in the better ones.*

I'm sure there were moments in that darkness where my dad couldn't see the light at the end of the tunnel. He probably didn't even know that it was a tunnel. It probably felt more like a bottomless pit. But when you hit what feels like rock bottom, the only way you can go is up. You can't fall any farther. And that's where Jesus met him, at the bottom. He picked him back up. He gave him hope again.

You see, the Jesus I know is in the business of redemption. No situation (that's no situation, just so we're clear) is too bleak for Him to shine some hope into. There is literally nothing that can't be redeemed by the love of Jesus. And that thought still sobers me, in the best way, to this day.

***Jesus knew how my dad felt about Thursdays.***

**He knew. *Every detail.***

For my Dad, Thursdays were the darkest day of the week. But for Jesus, it was the brightest opportunity to shine some hope into a bleary situation. If you haven't added the two together yet, the fact that my sister and I were both born on a Thursday was way more significant than I ever knew. Thursdays were the day my dad lost someone he loved so dearly. But this is a great example of Jesus bringing back double what the enemy had taken. Jesus looked at the loss in my Dad's life, and decided that he needed a double portion of joy, my sister and I, to replace what he'd lost. (And I am a joy. There's no doubt about that.)

I think that's pretty cool.

*Why have I told you this story?* If there's one thing I've learned since embarking on the adventure of writing, it's that the best way for your work to connect with others is to share your story. I want you to understand me as a person, and where I'm coming from. *I'm Ed. Nice to meet you.*

Before I even realised it, I was aware of emotional health, and over the years I've grown to understand what that actually means. My start in life was born out of a heart of redemption, although I didn't know it at the time. My entry to this world was part of Jesus healing my Dad's heart. And it continued with the addition of my sister three years later. Emotional healing has been part of who I am since birth. That's why I feel obligated to share my testimony. Join me on this journey, and you'll find that knowing yourself will help you with self control. Because if you can take care of you, then there really is no limit to what you can accomplish.

*So let's crack on.* I'm not getting any younger here.

# MASCULINITY: INSIDE AND OUT

Modern society is awash with various different tools to perform mass sensory overload. If you happen to find yourself wandering around Times Square or its not—so—twin brother, Leicester Square, you'll notice you are constantly bombarded with images. Images that are moving, still images that almost make you believe they're alive, images that are suggestive in nature; advertising for days. These images appeal to every emotion within you. The power of suggestion is ripe.

And there you find yourself in overload city. It's as if your entire body is having a party all at once, and it doesn't know how to cope with what's going on.

We're constantly being presented with things to ease our inhibitions. The latest fashion sense will cure that itch to be noticed. Owning that car will *surely* give you that standing you desire, now you can be part of the status quo! The beautiful irony in this is that so many people are striving to be original that they're actually becoming the same as everyone else. Everyone is trying to conform to their own image of social normality. And in that struggle to conform, we're in danger of quashing our own originality.

As a guy, I've grown up being presented with this image of what it means to be a man, and this isn't some image that's been influenced by what I've seen replicated through my family. By that I mean that there can be something greater than your own genetic input that seems to dictate what type of person you can become.

Being part of the most connected generation ever means that we also have more input in our lives, and from more sources than ever before. I've grown up with a pretty good understanding of who I am, and why I am the way I am. Not just because Eminem wrote a song about that.

Society's input on life has been huge. Everything from my music tastes and my fashion sense to how I interact with people: So many of my choices are determined by what I see and experience around me. I'm definitely one for soaking up new cultural excitement. The latest fad? If I can sense some relevance to me, I'm all about it. It's part of that innate desire to be connected to people.

*"If I follow this trend, does that make me just another face in the crowd, or am I embracing my own individuality as well?"*

The influence of the media on my life is so obvious to me, especially since I love creativity. I'm a musician. It's a massive part of who I am, and as such I'm always on the look out for the new and exciting sounds that artists are developing. In fact, I tend to spend too much money on music.

The challenge in being influenced by so many things is remembering to just be ourselves. We have to set the boundaries on what that looks like, otherwise we risk becoming part of the flooded crowd. The real fun is in taking the parts you love the most from society, and adding them to your life, just enough to make them your own, but not to the extent that you lose your originality.

For all the positive things that you can absorb from culture, there are certainly some negatives that counteract the joy they bring. This is not me wallowing or being consumed by the negative things, but more so being aware of them. As humans, we can be so easily influenced, and whatever you feed yourself is often what you replicate. Your outer world is so often a reflection of your inner world.

As a man, I've had so many different messages thrown at me regarding who I am, who I should be and what I should be enjoying. They affect even the simplest things, like who your friends should be and why.

*"Mate, you can't be friends with them. That's the*

*wrong crowd for you. Do they even like you? Are you into what they're into?"*

*"They're the cool kids. Are you popular enough to be in their group?"*

*"You're better than them. And you know it. Don't be seen with them. Your street cred will suffer, mate."*

You get the idea. In fact, most of you reading this probably know those internal monologues back to front. I know I'm not the only one who's experienced them.

The choices presented to guys are, I'm sure, many of the same ones presented to girls as well. I'm not about to separate the two and say I know this struggle more because I'm a guy. That is simply **not true.** What I do know is that the challenges I've faced in tackling my identity as a man are supremely important to how men are perceived in society, and as such these need to be talked about.

From a young age, I've been flooded with ideas of what it looks like to 'be a man'. What you watch, whom you interact with, what you wear, what websites you visit (you probably didn't think we'd be going there. We will), what you eat, etcetera, etcetera. It's a never—ending assault on the senses.

I grew up on Power Rangers, Teenage Mutant Ninja Turtles and Pokémon cards. Yeah, cards. Before 'Go' was even a thought.

Life was so much simpler then. I didn't have to figure out what to do with my life, or who I was. I could just simply enjoy the 90s for the glorious decade that they were. Being a kid was great. *Then you grow up*, and you are bombarded with messages left, right and centre.

In amongst trying to figure out what you believe, why you believe it and what you should do with your life, you're presented with so many options of what is possible that it can just become a little bit overwhelming. And it can cause you to just shut down. You shut down to the point where you're not even aware that you're doing it. That was my experience, and it's more common than you might think.

I've been blessed by having great friends in my life, friends who care enough to call me back to reality when I get lost in my own little world. They're not afraid to ask me the tough questions, champion me and bring out the best in me.

Let's say something somewhere in your day goes wrong, and you don't realise it, but your brain just flicks a switch. You immediately go from being invested in people or situation to suddenly not caring anymore. But everything still feels normal.

*"That's just how they are"*
*"My expectations of today were just too high".*
*"It's fine. No honestly. Nothing's wrong."*

These were all classic reasonings that I used to justify how I was feeling. Maybe you hold really high expectations in life (I do), and you discover it's near impossible to reach those expectations. **So you begin to form opinions of people, places, things.**

In actuality, this way of thinking is numbing your awareness of reality. It's putting harmful expectations on the people and places you encounter. We tend to think if we hide away, there's less of a chance to be hurt by something or someone. And getting hurt is painful.

How am I actually tying this into what it's like to be a man? I'm glad you asked. Just in case I followed a rabbit hole too far.

Well, men generally aren't expected to be the most emotionally aware half of humanity. At least, that's the story that I've seen unfold over my lifetime. It's the image society has given me.

**To be a man means you're strong — you're hard. You're powerful.**

**You're in control.**
**You provide.**
**You have responsibilities that don't enable you to be vulnerable.**
**You can't drop the facade.**

Weakness isn't acceptable. In fact, it's frowned upon. Because if you're seen as weak, who's going to be the strong one?

There's a huge market in portraying men as indestructible forces of nature that have no cracks in their armour. You see it in the film industry. Many films are geared around the strength of a man. Action movies usually have the alpha male figure somewhere near the top of the food chain, as a main character.

Usually, films with male leads that could be perceived as overly emotional or 'weak' (thinking along the lines of *The Notebook*) are just swept under the rug as something that a 'real man' would never watch, because emotions are dumb. Grr. I'd rather crack a beer can over my head than cry at something. MEN! *insert flex here*

Unfortunately, what I've seen this ethos create is a world where men are not engaged in what's actually going on with them. That's what culture has given us.

*The man that wears his heart on his sleeve is a minority.*

He's a minority because if you wear your heart on your sleeve, your emotions are never more than an arm's length away. And for most of us, that's a little too close. What this has created is the man that appears strong on the outside, but his inner world is in disarray.

By creating an image of a man that has it all together (because he appears strong and courageous on the outside) we've neglected to address whether he's actually aware of what's going on inside of him. If you're taught to just bottle feelings and emotions because showing them presents weakness, you're creating a ticking time bomb of emotional distress that could explode at likely the most inconvenient moment. *Which isn't good.*

The beautiful and somewhat tragic irony here is that society is pushing a heightened ability to be aware of everything around you, and take it all in. But in actuality we might be missing what's going inside of us. **And that's far more important.**

If we're not aware of ourselves, we can't be fully engaged with the rest of the world. We might think that we are. We might think that we don't need to engage with every emotion going on, give it some air or let it breathe in order to function successfully as a normal human. But then, if

Jesus gave us our emotions, then surely that doesn't look like shutting them down when we don't want to deal with them.

The reason I'm focusing on what it looks like to be a man dealing with self—awareness and emotion is a) because I am one, and b) no else is talking about it.

I'm aware that in modern society the parameters of gender is a very relevant topic, and the conversation on that is constantly moving and changing. Boundaries and expectations are being stretched all the time, which can be healthy in some circumstances. We live in the most 'metrosexual' generation in recent history. We are veering away from the stereotypes of men being the hunter—gatherer, the neanderthal—like provider. Instead, we're starting to see them as people who are more in touch with their feminine side.

*Hear what I'm saying here, and not what I'm* ***not.***

It doesn't matter to me which side of the supposed 'spectrum' of manliness you feel like you fall. In my opinion, neither is right or wrong. To me, the modus operandi has to be to "love everyone". That's our commission. There's no judgement here. If there was, I wouldn't be modelling Jesus very well, would I? What I am seeking to do is combat the myth that in order to be a man, you can't be in touch with your emotions.

# TIN MAN

Ever had someone tell you to "man up"? I have. In fact, it's an internal monologue that I've heard countless times. The back and forth is constant, and the internal fight can be both exhausting and depressing. You see, long before we had to combat the messages being thrown at us by society regarding our emotional intelligence, we already had a discussion going through our minds. If all you've ever known is being told that your emotions are bad, and that you shouldn't really give them space to breathe or allow them to exist, then why on earth would you want to confront them?

It's taken me quite a few years to understand that my emotions are actually here to help me function as a normal human being. I've had to relearn important thought processes that affect how I approach emotions. There were things that I've learned over the years that certainly didn't help. Those internal monologues that I mentioned are prime examples of some of the thought processes I have encountered when confronting my own emotions. I think, as a guy, I've been saturated with this idea that being in touch with your emotions is probably the weakest thing you can do. Take crying, for example. It isn't really seen as a manly or macho thing to cry. It isn't even close to that persona. It's almost like we steer so far away from embracing that level of vulnerability that we forget how to do it.

Now, I know I'm painting a very broad picture here, and not all men are like this. I know this to be true because I have men in my life that have taught me to embrace vulnerability. It's also possible that my own emotional awareness has come from being surrounded by a lot of women during my lifetime. Before you create an assumption, let me unpack that a little for you.

I've always known and experienced a large feminine influence in my life, as I have three sisters. I think is a big part of why I am the way that I am (soon, I'll have to give Eminem royalties). It feels as though I've managed to stay away (mostly) from this false notion that men can't be emotional, or vulnerable. *At least, it **had** felt that way until the last few years.* (I hasten to add here, this is a cultural stigma that I've experienced, and so I'm not trying to make judgements.)

**Emotions are good. They're important. They have a huge influence on your health.**

Everything made sense, but everything changed a couple of years ago.

You see, I was completely fine with embracing emotions when they led to positive outcomes. I think everyone is, to be honest. It's the easy route. Nobody has to get hurt that way; If only life was as simple as just dealing in positivity and good emotions. But when it came to pain, I didn't want anything to do with it. Because I knew that it would hurt. I definitely didn't want to encounter that, or let it become real. I think most people are quite good at suppressing pain so it doesn't become real. In reality, that is far more damaging.

My viewpoint on emotions changed very quickly when I experienced pain and emotional turmoil, and it wasn't a life—altering amount of pain by any means. I know a lot of people experience that, and I'm thankful that I haven't had to live it out. To those that have, I have so much admiration and respect for how you pick yourselves back up so as not to let a situation or circumstance define you.

The pain I experienced was just enough for me to notice it. Just enough to be real. However, when it came to tackling what was lying at the root of the pain, that wasn't an option for me. That was too vulnerable. I didn't want to go there. At least that way it was just a figment of my imagination, right?

**Wrong.**

Often we find it easier to nurse and feed the fear we're harbouring, rather than outing it as the lie that it is. Because, for some of us, we've fed it for so long that it actually feels like our reality. And when you're in a situation, it can be very hard to see it from the outside. *Perspective is everything.*

But fear is simply that; fear. It's illogical in its very existence, especially to a follower of Jesus. You either believe that He defeated every sin, fear and discrepancy on the cross, or you don't.

For me, it was much easier to gloss over what I was feeling with the classic responses I wanted to present to everyone around me that I was doing "just fine, thanks". This kept everyone at a distance that I could manage, and I was happy with that. *Happy in my own misery* (If that isn't an album title for an emo band, I don't know what is). I was keeping everything at a safe distance, my friends, my family and my emotions. Except in this case, the word 'safe' is ironic in its use. I was so terrified of encountering and embracing pain (which would lead to healing, just to brighten this story up a little) that I was closing myself off to everyone and everything, and not being safe at all. But on the outside, everything seemed "just fine".

*My belief system was backwards.*

In so many ways, I was experiencing the opposite of the freedom that I know Jesus gives. The voice of fear inside my head was far more prevalent than that of the One who brings life. ***Side note:*** *If you feel like your life is being governed by a voice that causes you to feel uneasy and anxious, that voice doesn't belong to your Heavenly Father. God only wants the best for His kids and only operates out of love towards them.* I was experiencing the opposite of freedom because of my inability to be aware of what was going on inside of me. And when you operate only out of what you're feeling (whether you realise it or not), it's really unhealthy. Incidentally, I don't believe that emotions should govern you or dictate how you live your life. I do believe that they are an invaluable part of being human, and as such they need to be given the space to breathe, embraced and marvelled in. They need to be noticed and nurtured, otherwise you run the risk of selling yourself short to everyone around you. You're not fully you if you're not aware of what's going on inside.

As my journey progressed, I became trapped in my own thought processes, and it wasn't benefitting me or anyone around me. "Self—Protect Mode" was in full swing, but I couldn't see it happening. Thankfully, I had people in my life that cared about me enough to draw me out of the mire when I set up camp there.

But not everyone does. So this is a rallying call to the guys reading this. Just because you might have heard a message that you're not supposed to feel anything, doesn't mean that it's true. If the general consensus isn't to engage with your emotions, the barometer is way off kilter. ***Feeling is a good thing.*** That might make controversial reading to some of you. **Good.**

If you're not feeling, then you're not really living. You can't truly experience the highs and lows of what it really means to be human. You can't revel fully in the victories, and you certainly can't experience the pain of defeat that actually allows you to grow. Guys, contrary to popular opinion, being sensitive is actually a good thing.

*"Wait...what? *cracks beer can*"*

Sensitivity is not only a necessary part of the vulnerability you need to have fulfilling relationships, but it also allows you to be in tune with who God has created you to be. After all, how are we supposed to experience the revelatory love of Jesus and what that truly means to us if we can't even shed a tear? I don't actually think that's possible. Jesus meets us in our vulnerability. He hangs out in the most painful places we know. That issue you don't want to confront because it seems too raw? Jesus is waiting there to catch you when you collapse. That thing that you feel like there's no coming back from? Jesus is there. He's already paved the road on the hill to your comeback. He'll be behind you pushing when you feel like you've got nothing left.

**That's the Jesus I know and love.**

I found Him in the most painful places in my life. He was there when it felt like He couldn't possibly be there, because how can anyone save me from that grief?

Earlier in this book, I mentioned the redemption that Jesus unfolded in my Dad's life by way of bringing love to a situation where it seemed love and hope had vanished. The wonderful thing about my King is that He doesn't just show up when we need Him to (although sometimes it can feel like that). He's there all the time. Sometimes we just need to adjust our perspective to see Him. Desperation creates a dependency that human nature cannot control, like a void that cannot be filled. The only one that can fix that brokenness is Jesus. He operates from a level of love that is incomprehensible to the human mind. Where logic states that it can't be done, Jesus is there counteracting that very thought process. He is the God of the impossible, the One who makes miracles seem normal. How wonderful that He wants to meet us in our most broken state, and bring us into wholeness once again? That's the kind of love that will take a lifetime to wrap your head around. And even then, we still won't fully grasp it. It's a good job we've got eternity together to marvel at that wonder.

Emotions are not just good, they're great. And the sooner we men realise that, the better. Because currently we are just presenting 50% of ourselves to those around us if we're not in tune with our inner workings and feelings. I think this revelation is rooted in how deep your grasp of the love of Jesus is for you. If you don't feel like you can share everything with the one who shared it all for you, then why would you view being vulnerable as a good thing? It takes a level of appreciation for what He did for us to be able to understand that He wants us to live in that same level of intimacy with everyone around us.

Maybe you didn't see vulnerability modelled in the home in which you grew up. Maybe there wasn't a father figure there that cried in front of his kids and his wife. Instead, he just kept it bottled up inside. Or perhaps he elicited anger towards those closest to him. If you can relate to that, I'm sorry for how difficult that might have been. But I have good news. There's a new model for weakness that actually looks like strength to those who can see it. And he goes by the name of Jesus. He gave literally *everything* so that you could live in fullness, in every area of your life.

The only catch? You need to embrace brokenness, vulnerability, weakness — basically anything that makes you scared when it comes to emotions. Why? Simply because He loves you enough to meet you in the midst of your anguish. If we're not in tune with the most broken parts of ourselves, we risk ignoring the potential revelation those same areas can bring when we show them to Jesus.

You see guys, Jesus is the solution to the emotional dilemma plaguing society. We just have our perception of what it means to be a man backwards. He should be the benchmark for manhood. He modelled stability whilst embracing brokenness. His weaknesses were often the source of His greatest strength. Because the Father filled in the blanks.

That same grace is available to us.

*But we can't duck and run for cover when it starts hurting.* Don't build walls around pain, because you'll create a house with no stability in the foundations. One day it'll fold like a deck of cards. And probably when you least expect it. ***Be aware of what you're feeling, and feel it.*** If you don't, you risk becoming a robot. And even the Tin Man needed a heart in the end.

# ME SO NEEDY

Growing up in Britain has taught me a thing or three about expressing how I'm doing, what's going on with me, and figuring out if anyone actually cares enough to listen.

It's interesting to notice the cultural differences in a few of the places I've visited in my lifetime. Americans love to interact in a way that Brits often find terrifying — with a sense of excitement and genuineness rather than a sarcastic comment. In fact, I think everyone I've encountered in other countries has been willing to engage in some form of communication simply because it's seen as a nice and normal thing to do with one another.

I've had to combat the withdrawal mentality that I see so often in British society, and to be honest I'm not a fan of it whatsoever. Somehow we've created this society where isolation has become the norm, and people tend to think they are better off because of it.

I'm all for understanding the differences between introverts and extroverts. It took me a good few years to learn that you can be both if you want to be. I know I definitely have the characteristics of both, and I'm totally fine with that, but the danger comes when we decide to let those labels define who we are when it might not be who we are at all.

Introverts tend to need time by themselves to recharge, whilst extroverts are often the opposite. For introverts, quietness is often their friend. Extroverts find that people bring them life, and they thrive in social settings where they can draw upon other people and at the same time give a part of themselves to that setting. But it is important to note that there's a big difference between *introversion* and *isolation*. An *introvert* can be healthy when managed the right way, whereas *isolation* can cause a lot of issues if you're not switched on. In my opinion, this understanding seems to have been lost a bit in modern society.

I'm a big fan of both of these types of people. I see the characteristics of both in not only myself but also those closest to me. It's easy to point at someone and guess what type of person they could be, or make an assumption. But how many people just live under the blanket definition of what a test or other people might have told them?

*Here's what I'm getting at — you have to know the*

*difference between who people say you're supposed to be, and who you really are.* Being a "needy" person is generally considered a bad thing. That's largely because the phrase 'need' has been drastically misinterpreted and painted in a bad light. When I used to think of having 'needs', it immediately presented me with a terrifying thought of being a burden on someone; that someone else would feel weighed down by me expressing things that are actually vital to my normal function as a human.

**And why is that?** I've come to experience something that could perhaps be best described as 'emotionless society'. Get your pitchforks ready. It's about to go down.

Brits are seemingly emotionless for the most part, mainly deadpan and hugely sarcastic in our response to pretty much everything. Incidentally, I love sarcasm, but isn't it easy to think that way about ourselves? It's so easy to place a negative stereotype upon ourselves, and not give it a second thought. That's certainly cause for concern.

An 'emotionless society' is an easy description to grasp because it suggests that nobody's showing what's actually going on within them. It feels intrusive and like we're overstepping the mark with someone if we actually stop them in the street to see how their day is going, and none of us want to be stopped by those people on the high street because we're either in too much of a rush, or we just can't be bothered to engage. This is a harsh but true summary in my opinion, and I know because I've felt it.

Have you ever stopped to think that by stopping for that conversation in the street, your day could take a turn for the better? Have you considered that by sharing your life with someone else, in that split—second moment, you might change their day for the better as well?

I know that it's really easy to talk about this stuff, and not actually follow up with it. And this is as much a challenge for myself as it is for anyone reading this. If we are to stop and engage with people, we might just pick up something that we've been missing that day. Maybe all you've needed that day is to communicate something you've been thinking about with someone else, and this is your first and perhaps only opportunity to do that. I'm not saying that we all need to become best friends with everyone we meet (although that might be fun) and share everything that's going on in our lives, but by embracing conversation with someone when you don't really feel like it, you might actually find that you're meeting a need that'll make your day that much better.

Emotional disconnect often happens because we aren't aware of our needs. That same disconnect that prevented you from engaging in conversation with someone you care about is the same that leads you past meaningful conversations with someone in the street might just need one.

Sometimes, the pain of no connection can be easier to embrace than the challenge of being connected, you will always have to invest something worthwhile to become connected. Separation can be simple, but embracing someone and everything they bring with them can be difficult. Isolation is easy to embrace because it involves a compromise of connection. If you've always assumed that connection equals pain then why on earth would you want to fight for it? If you think that the closer you get to someone, the more likely you are to be hurt, then it's totally understandable that you wouldn't seek connection and intimacy with someone.

I want to counter this way of thinking with something so simple that it seems incredibly obvious. Disconnection, connection, discomfort, comfort, pain, happiness — all of these emotions are attached to needs. Those needs don't always have the same name as what you're feeling, but they affect *what* you feel.

I went from being someone who was completely averse to emotional engagement to someone who finally understood what it meant to address my needs. By addressing them, I began to live a much happier life. Being aware of one's needs and experiencing emotions as they happen are all connected.

If we could just obtain the simple skill of addressing our needs, I think we'd start to see a much healthier and happier society.

The fear of 'being needy' is probably the biggest thing that detracts us from us actually engaging with our needs. I know I have had to battle the mentality that being needy is a bad thing. Multiple times in my life, I've decided I'd much rather inconvenience myself by sacrificing something I need, rather than inconveniencing someone else to meet that need.

I once decided it would be easier to walk a mile and a half to get where I needed to go rather than ask a friend for a lift, because in my mind that would have been a massive strain on them. I didn't want to be a burden. The reality was quite the opposite. Because I was so scared of asking in the first place, I ignored a simple solution right in front of me. I decided I'd rather be stubborn and create more hassle for myself, than have the 'worry' of troubling someone else for something.

***Doesn't that all sound a bit ludicrous? Yet it's not uncommon.***

That definitely wasn't the only time I've had to combat that mentality. Somewhere along the line, that way of thinking has been engrained into me. *It's easier for me to make my own situation more difficult than ask for help.* And that's really what addressing your needs is all about; *asking for help.*

Our reality as believers is that we can't live our lives without the help of Jesus. We just can't. He changes the way we look at *everything*. I know that I certainly couldn't live my life effectively if I didn't have Him.

Jesus is the provider of all our needs. Otherwise, why would it say in scripture that He is all—sufficient? **If He can't provide for us in every area of lack, then either our mindset needs to change, or the scriptures are not true.** I know which one it is. He is "the author and perfector of our faith" (*Hebrews 12:2*) and I know that I'm constantly being perfected in my thinning. I trust His way far more than I trust my own; that's real dependency.

We have to combat this way of thinking, that we're too much for someone else, that we're too needy, that we're too demanding. They're all rooted in the same tree — a massive tree of lies. This way of thinking is always going to separate us from our intended design to live in intimacy with Jesus and those closest to us. The enemy loves to get in and stick his foot in the door between you and Jesus, casually throwing some lies in as though they were normal conversation. **Being needy can be a good thing.** *It's the* *mindset surrounding it that needs to shift.*

When we start looking at being needy as a good thing, and begin addressing our needs in a healthy way, then its perception as a negative thing will change, and we'll remain true to our DNA.

Needs are a beautiful thing because they constantly challenge you to grow into the best you can be. When tackled in a positive way, they empower you. They make you stronger. They make you more emotionally stable.

If you can learn to embrace and deal with your needs in an affirming manner, you're a huge leap towards being everything that Jesus intends you to be.

# GREAT EXPECTATIONS

Growing up in British society can stifle you, somewhat. There are many wonders and bonuses to being a Brit, but sadly there is also a sense that we must keep ourselves grounded with our expectations. If we don't, we're in danger of being too lackadaisical and free—spirited, and therefore not rooted in reality.

I've been fortunate enough to spend a fair amount of time in the United States at various points in my life, and one thing that is startlingly obvious is their positivity, their outlook on life. Try telling an American that the U.S. isn't the greatest country in the world, and you'll likely find yourself in for a long conversation that will result in circles being paced with no end in sight. I love how much they love their own country. I actually feel like we can learn a little from their zealous nature. After all, the United Kingdom was once a powerful and inspiring nation to many, and shouldn't we be proud and excited about the home that we represent?

It took me a little longer to understand just how wonderful my home country is. I needed to remove myself from my home to fully appreciate what I had. But now that my perspective has shifted in terms of how I view my home, and the gratitude I have for the freedom afforded here, it makes our reserved approach to expectations much more complicated.

***Unmet expectations can mess you up.***

I've encountered the challenge of having high expectations in many different areas of my life and in many different circumstances. Perhaps my expectations are high simply because people tell me to be realistic, and I refuse to listen. Here's a newsflash: realistic expectations and small dreams rarely change the world. If you want to change the face of the planet, you need to dream bigger than what you yourself can accomplish. If we're not pushing the boundaries of what we deem is possible, we're not giving Jesus much room to move in our lives. That's why it's called faith; because you know you can't do everything on your own.

Dreaming small is not a bad thing, but it's important to be pushing yourself in what you expect God can do in your life. As long as small dreams are helping to facilitate bigger ones, or challenge you to create bigger ones, then they're completely within their place. Dreams that scare you aren't necessarily a bad thing.

They should be big enough to make you question whether they are even attainable because I've found that's often where God wants to show up, and show you what he can do.

So we find ourselves back at **the wonders of met expectations.**

Having expectations is wonderful because it means you're looking for the good in a situation. I associate the term 'expectation' with positivity, but obviously it can be associated with negativity as well. One, however, is life—giving and one is not. If you spend most of your time thinking that things are going to go wrong in your life, and are constantly looking for the negative in situations, then your life is going to be pretty miserable. I believe that Jesus wants the best for my life, and has the biggest dreams and expectations for me, but I can't believe for that with a negative outlook on life. If I did, I would be stifling the ability of the Holy Spirit to move in my life.

Sometimes we need to shift our own paradigm in order to allow God to move more freely in our lives. And, just in case you were wondering, that can feel uncomfortable. Discomfort is not a bad thing, as it can often be right in front of breakthrough. We just can't see the breakthrough because we're too focused on the pain and discomfort we're experiencing. Let's use some practical examples to break this down.

As a millennial, one of the things I'm most often confronted with in going for job interviews and job applications is a 'lack of experience'. It seems as if some employers want you to have 45 years of experience at 29 years of age. It can be quite demoralising, and a person can sometimes fail to get off the starting block when searching for employment. But if we all believed that we weren't qualified enough to make it in society, then we'd all just be sitting at home feeling sorry for ourselves. I'm pretty sure most of the people you look up to and admire in society didn't let their own limitations quash their ability to dream big.

When approaching that scenario (job applications), I could choose to look at it in one of two ways. I could choose to see it from a defeatist mindset, and count myself out of the running before I've begun to walk. Or, I could look at it from the perspective that only Jesus can give, which is that you don't need to be qualified to fulfil your destiny. In fact, it can be the least qualified people that impact those around them the most.

If I go into that job interview with a positive mindset, geared towards expecting success, then I'm in a much better headspace. If I go into that interview with my head hung low because of how I view myself and my life (I expect the negative in life), I'm not likely to impress those who are in the position to provide me with a stepping stone towards my own growth. To me, it's a no brainer as to what is the more exciting and challenging option, and the one that can bear the most fruit.

**Now let's apply the wonders of expectation to relationship.** *Now we're getting real.* Expectations in relationships can be deadly, if you're not good at managing them, and especially if you're not good at processing emotions. I say this as someone who has learned how important it is to be able to do both of those well, but I'm also preaching to myself here. In my mind, there are two main types of relationships. There are relationships you have with friends and those closest to you, e.g., family. And then there are relationships in a romantic context with another person. Either one of these can provide you with great joy, and great pain.

Here's a practical example of how I approach expectation in friendship. We've all got that one friend who is pretty unreliable in getting back to you. As a person who holds high expectations of the relationships in my life, I often find myself walking an emotional tightrope in terms of what I expect from other people. Let's say I want to meet up with this person regularly because I value their role in my life and want them to speak into my world. But like I said, they don't have a good record of fulfilling my expectations for what this friendship should look like.

*I hasten to add here, that unless you communicate your expectations with the other person in this situation, you're likely to be disappointed most of the time, because, sadly, people aren't mind—readers.*

We agree to meet at 5 and they don't show until 6. By then it's too late. They constantly reschedule on you, most of the time at the last minute. In this scenario, it can be very easy to form opinions of someone and start to see them through a jaded lens.

"Oh, that's just who they are. They can't really help that."

"I never really expect much from them to be honest. They've let me down too many times now."

Before you realise it, you've formulated a judgement in your head (and heart) as to who this friend is to you, and more importantly you begin to place your negative expectation of that person onto others.

This is a classic example of expecting someone to be something that they're actually not. In this case, the 'expectation' is that they're a disappointment, because that's what you've experienced. So you're making judgements based upon the hurt you've felt.

**A dangerous road, folks.**

Most of the time, this happens because there's been no communication when someone has experienced disappointment. Then lies creep in and roots go down. Whether you realised it or not, your thought process towards someone has shifted to expect the worst of them. You find it difficult to associate positivity when you think of them, because you're so used to being let down. The simple solution here is to talk to the other person in this equation. You might be pleasantly surprised by how much a simple conversation can change relationships.

I share this, because I've learned to change the way I approach expectations with the people close to me. I've learned that communicating your hurt to someone you've felt aggrieved by can change your entire relationship. There's always room to give people more grace for just ***being human.***

It's so easy to forget that humans are fallible beings, and as such are prone to making mistakes. The danger comes when you expect people to hurt you. Then the onus has been placed on *your* expectations.

Most of the time, we just need to allow people a little room to breathe and make mistakes so that they can learn and grow. In the meantime, we can learn how to deal with our own views of people and manage our own expectations. High expectations are wonderful, but you must learn to deal with disappointment if and when it rears its head. Otherwise you risk walking down the broken paving slab road to negativity.

So, now on to the fun part — **expectation in romantic relationships.** I say it's a fun part (somewhat ironically) because it's something I've encountered countless times, and had to deal with. Expectations are a wonderful thing when it comes to romantic relationships. You should have them, so that there's vision in the relationship.

I, myself, am a *massive romantic.*

This has led me to both wonderful ideas and dramatic, often painful, conclusions. I dream big when it comes to love, as I believe anyone should. The primary reason for this is that romantic relationships are very close to my heart, and one of the things that I desire the most in my life. It means getting to share your journey with someone, writing your own story together as you both turn the pages. However, this road has also led me to experience a fair amount of pain in not dealing with my expectations correctly, or in a healthy manner.

One of the most profound things I've ever heard spoken about healthy relationships is that *your intimacy level should always match your commitment level.* The reason this is so profound to me is that I've lived out situations where that has not been the case, and subsequently I've had to pick up the pieces of my own heart and piece it back together again. I'm not saying it was anybody else's fault (although let's be honest, it takes two to tango), but I was not aware, in the moment, of the intensity of my own emotions. In turn, this led me to blur the commitment and intimacy levels in my head.

I can recall a few instances in my life where my expectations of a relationship were not the same as the other person involved. I might expect someone to be available at the end of the phone whenever I need them, but they might not hold the same expectation of our relationship. How is the other person in a relationship supposed to know what you expect from them if you don't communicate it to them? This is why communication is so important.

High expectations in romantic relationships are commonplace for me, because I like to dream big and hope for the best. However, I've learnt in the last couple of years that it is so important to manage your expectations in a healthy way. Maintain those high levels of anticipation for greatness in your life, but **do not** shy away from dealing with disappointment when it comes trying to kick you in the face.

*And it will.*

I can tell you from my own experience that pushing through the pain is worth the momentary turmoil you might feel. Disappointment thrives in the hearts of those that dream big and come up short. Instead of choosing to bury that feeling of pain, try persevering through the hard process towards your own breakthrough. On the other side of that supposed emptiness is actually a freedom greater than you can ever anticipate. *Jesus is in the business of restoring broken people to newer, fuller, better, happier versions of themselves.*

Heartbreak doesn't have to last nearly as long as people think it does. I realise that this might be a controversial sentence, and that everyone has their own process when it comes to dealing with a broken heart. I'm not negating that at all. But I would like to propose that too often we spend time hanging out with sadness, brokenness, and pain because they provide us with a sense of false comfort. It can be easier to spend time with those difficult emotion because they can't let you down twice. You become comfortable with them. But there's another way. There's a Comforter who actually wants to comfort us in our pain, heartache and heartbreak. ***The question isn't "How long will this feeling last?" but "How long will I build a fortress around my pain to protect the status quo, rather than letting Jesus in to help me heal?"***

Jesus wants to meet us in our most vulnerable places, to provide us with stability that only He can provide. When we let Him in to shore up the foundations, we set ourselves up with a healthy base for future relationships because we're not dependant on other people to fill the emptiness. Instead, we have a Saviour there who is ever—reliable, and won't leave us high and dry in the emotions department. Sometimes you just need to let yourself feel it all. *Everything. All the emotions.* Sometimes you need to let them all out, in order to bring life back in.

*Unfulfilled expectations only carry negative influence when you let disappointment creep in and make a home.*

Perhaps that situation with that girl didn't play out how you wanted it to; don't sit and stew over hurt feelings. Instead, feel what's going on, embrace it and kick disappointment in the face with powerful decision making that allows you to find stability.

***If you let it, a lie can step in and influence every decision you ever make.*** I know this, because I've done it.

Without even realising it, at some point in my life I had adopted the belief that I was never truly going to find happiness, and to me that looked like I was never getting married. As a massive romantic, you can understand why this is such a damaging lie to believe. The sad thing was I knew I was listening to (and feeding) that lie every day. But instead of dealing with it by bringing it to Jesus, I decided to ignore it and let it fester. It turned into a ticking time bomb to bring into any future romantic relationship. That belief would slowly but surely eat away at any potential success I could have in a relationship.

When I finally decided to show my vulnerability to Jesus, He showed me that I had nothing to be afraid of in the first place. He's always on the look out for our hearts. He wants us to be whole and healthy. Dislodging that lie was as simple as surrendering my fear and giving it to Jesus and allowing Him to show me the truth. The beautiful truth was that I could have a successful relationship, like everyone else. But it took me surrendering my limited understanding before I could find the truth in the situation.

Expectations only have as much influence as you allow them to have, which can be a lot when you're a dreamer. The important thing is to not ignore the beauty of the process — be it pain or success.

***Our vulnerabilities are a beautiful thing. We have to learn to view them that way, otherwise we don't truly love ourselves.*** Don't be afraid of expectation, commitment, brokenness (or anything I've listed at some point in this chapter). Although those things may seem daunting, you are called to walk in an authority that means you don't succumb to hurt and pain, but rather live out of a wholeness that impacts those around you. *Expect greatness, and* ***expect the unexpected.*** *Often, that's where the best surprises are found.*

# EMPTY WORDS

Since I was younger, I've been interested in words, the meaning that they carry and how they influence the lives we lead. Over the years, I've become better at communicating with those around me. That's largely due to the fact that I often think through what I'm about to say before the words come out of my mouth. I know the importance of words, so there's a lot of thought that goes into choosing the ones I feel carry the most weight. I take great pride in my ability to get across exactly what I mean by thinking a great deal before sharing. Communication has always been a very important thing to me, because I understand the value it carries. The reason I'm writing this book is because I believe I have something important to say.

That hasn't been the easiest place to get to, believe me. As with any creative person, we are always our own worst critic. So when we actually choose to believe in ourselves, that's half the battle won. I believe that everyone carries their own individual message to share with the world, and for me it happens to be the topic of communication.

*I can't stress how important the concept of good communication is within the confines of any relationship.* The words you say carry weight and authority, whether you're aware of it or not. So whatever you're creating with the words that are coming out of your mouth, be aware that they have an impact greater than you can fathom.

I've realised recently that there is a massive difference between having a theoretical approach to something, and actually being in it and making conscious choices that dictate an outcome.

***So, what does communication really bring to the table in a relationship?***

The truth is that communication truly defines our friendships, romantic relationships, and familial relationships. The way in which you communicate with someone often defines how they see you, and how they receive what you say.

I mentioned earlier that people are not mind—readers. I've witnessed it so many times — the expectation that someone else just 'knows' what you're thinking or feeling. And then there's the annoyance that might follow when the other person doesn't understand why he or she is upset.

It's become such a pervasive mentality that there are now whole perceptions built around this concept. For instance, there's the stereotype that says women are impossible to read, too complicated, and too complex. (I don't subscribe to this notion, just to clear that up, for any female readers that immediately wanted to throw this book across the room…)

And then there's the supposed understanding of men — that they're really basic creatures who just don't know what's going on around them.

These societal tropes are built upon the idea that communication isn't as necessary (as it is) in forming healthy, long—lasting relationships, yet *without good communication your relationship is never really going to get out of the starting blocks.*

There are many of us who can communicate quite well, but there's a difference between 'quite well' and actually what's truly going on inside of us.

***"How's it going?"***
***(Inner world in chaos)…"Fine thanks!"***

Obviously I'm not just talking about surface level conversation here, although that's a part of it. What I'm really getting at is the narrative that goes on behind the scenes, in people's heads. The one that others rarely see. It's so easy to present a façade to those around us that says we're completely fine. I've encountered a few people in my lifetime that would consider themselves professionals at that, but they're actually just mastering the ability to hide what's actually going on within them.

*It's easy to say things without actually saying anything at all.* Sometimes, words are just that; words. They're used as fillers, and sometimes we don't really mean anything we're saying. The challenge lies in how to decipher what people truly mean, and what they are communicating. If you can sift through the filler and bravado that's all too common, then you can get to the root of what's actually going on.

The reason this hits home so well for me is that for years, I was a master of this art. I was the feelings ninja. I could mask everything that was going on inside of me with a few simple short words: *"Fine thanks, how are you?"* I became so good at covering up how I was actually feeling that I didn't even realise I was doing it half of the time. That's when you know you've either become a master at your craft, or you've started drifting in to numbness. For me, it was often much easier to convey that simple response (or something similar) to people around me, because I didn't want to feel like I was burdening anyone with my issues.

***In reality this kind of thinking will only hurt us.***

By preventing myself from engaging with my emotions to this extent, I was actually just building a self—harming safety net for myself. In the moment it felt nice and safe, but that was only because I had become numb to the truth of what I was actually feeling. By keeping everyone at a distance, I believed I was in far less danger of being hurt. But when you genuinely love people and need them in your life to feel fully alive, shutting them out is going to lead to hurt anyway.

*My fear of vulnerability was actually rooted in my inability to let in the one who could comfort me the most —Jesus.*

I was good at keeping people at a distance, but that was only because I'd been doing it with Jesus for quite a while. The most distressing thing about it is that my nature is the complete opposite. Somewhere along the way I let a lie (or seven) seep in and distract my gaze from the One who deserves it. I had emotionally shut down the most vulnerable parts of my heart.

***You can now see why this was quite the sobering experience.***

I've learned that if you can't communicate honestly with those closest to you then it will be difficult to replicate any sort of intimacy with *anyone*. Your first line of communication is often the most important. If the line is frayed there, there's a good chance that the disconnect will trickle down and destroy the wires the further it goes.

The lack of communication in relationships can be quite startling. Whether you've experienced it first hand yourself, or witnessed it in others. If you're not talking about what's really going on inside of you, then you're not really connecting with those closest to you. It may not be easy to share your life with others, but it's part of being followers of Jesus.

I've also learned that you don't need to share everything with everyone all of the time. For someone who prioritises feeling connected to people, this can be quite a challenge. Countless instances can be recalled where the 'right' option for connection feels like telling everyone everything that's going on, however, this is not always the right solution. You get to choose what you relay and to whom. There's a lot of power in that choice. We are all responsible for safe—guarding our own hearts, and often the more people we let into the most vulnerable places, the higher the risk of getting hurt. This is a tension with which we need to learn to live, and we get to figure out what our own balance needs to be. It is possible to create a healthy balance, but not without being aware of how much you're giving to other people in that process.

***Letting everyone into every area of your life magnifies the possibility of losing your own voice.*** I've been in a position where I've been so heavily reliant on other people to give me input that it actually takes away from the trust I have in my own decisions. Quite often, the more people that speak into your life, the louder their voices become; to the detriment of your own. Don't let others drown out your ability to act out of the authority that Christ has bestowed upon you.

If we can relate this to romantic relationships, it starts to take the form of a co—dependence. Some of you might argue that a certain level of dependency is a good thing in relationships (and to an extent I would agree). However, when the relationship starts to become too dependent on one person, then you might be at risk of either a power trip, or one person not believing that they have the ability to make good decisions.

*Over-reliance on somebody is not just bad for you, but also for them.* If somebody has become a life—support to you, then it's highly probable that somewhere down the line too much responsibility has been placed on one person. In that circumstance, when the person who is providing the life support leaves, the other perishes. *That is a total lack of balance in a relationship.*

***The communication of expectations means that nobody is left in the dark as to what the other is feeling.***

I believe that this is often where the lack of balance in dependency is rooted. If you haven't communicated with your significant other what it is that you expect from them, in terms of commitment, or fulfilling basic needs then it can be very easy for them to assume a role that they think fills this blank space. In actuality, they are trying to compensate in an area that doesn't need any compensation, all because of a lack of simple communication.

If I communicate, "I expect this from you in our relationship," you then have the opportunity to get on board with that idea, or challenge it. You can tell me that it's completely unreasonable, and then we can decide how to move forward from there. In doing that, we eliminate the possibility for misunderstanding, and papering over the cracks with what we think might be the right solution.

Contrary to popular belief, confrontation can be a good and healthy antidote to a creaking (or perfectly healthy) relationship when done from a heart of always seeking to love the other person first.

I'm someone that often struggles with surface—level conversation because I want to *really* know how someone is doing. This has been a practice that I have had to work out.

If you're not letting the other half of the relationship know what's really going on with you, then you risk creating a disconnect, and things start to crack.

*A glass house built around your heart is still glass. It's susceptible to cracks, and fully transparent.*

***Honesty actually is the best policy.***

# ROSE-TINTED GLASSES

***"She's nothing like I expected."***
***"It's not quite what I imagined."***

To some, the sentences in bold could seem quite negative. You might read that under the pretence of the person in question not living up to someone else's expectations. Maybe they just don't quite 'fit the bill' for said person.

On the other side of the coin, both of those sentences can be taken in a highly positive manner. Maybe she's nothing like you expected because expectations can be a killer. Maybe she's actually more than you ever expected, and more than you could have ever imagined. Perhaps your expectations have been exceeded.

I often feel as though this way of thinking — searching out the positive in situations like is rare. It's so easy to search for the negative over the positive. Which, if that's the case, probably means you need to adjust your lens.

*What would happen if everyone approached relationships with an overarching sense of positivity, and high expectations for only the best of outcomes?*

I think the reason a lot of people approach relationships with a negative outlook is because they're not actually looking in the right direction. What I mean is their focus can so easily be upon what they want from said relationship. Now 'wants' are all well and good, and necessary things to have when pursuing someone for the goal of connection on a deep, heartfelt level. Humans are wired to want to be connected with one another in some form or another. That's why we seek out friends, to form community, and to feel a part of something bigger than just ourselves.

And when you apply that desire for connection to a romantic relationship, the want only grows deeper. The hunger is greater for deeper connection. We want to be understood and known at our very core. We want to trust someone with the innermost part of our hearts, and feel protected, valued and loved unconditionally. However, the danger comes when your 'wants' are dictated to you by society. I've already talked quite a bit about societal expectations on relationships, and how easy it is for us to be spoon—fed idealistic romanticism based upon somebody else's notion of what love is.

*Hollywood is brilliant at it.* I can attest to this, as I'm a true romantic who often feels hard done by the movie industry's ideas of 'love' and 'romance'. They are so far fetched that to obtain them feels like scaling Everest backwards with your eyes closed. If we all live out of the expectation that real love is only received and gained by following the path of a film adaptation, then we're going to realise very quickly that there needs to be space for disappointment in our lives. It's not that we expect it, but we know it *will* appear because our expectations are so high that they're nearly impossible to fulfil or exceed.

So in a society that feeds us ideas of what we think we **want** from relationships, how do we determine what it is that we actually want, and better yet figure out what we **need**?

Everybody has their own ideas of what they think they want in a relationship. Some of these expectations are reasonable, and some of them maybe warped through their own lens. In that sense, figuring out what you actually want is as much up to the individual as anything else.

What I'm not saying here is that expectations are a bad thing. It's definitely good to have them, but also to allow yourself to be moulded and changed by the other person in that relationship. And if you don't have expectations, then you're probably selling yourself short. If you understand your own self—worth it'll be much easier to feel 'ready' for a relationship.

So basically, you get to figure out what it is that you want from your relationships. **One bit of advice:** don't be too tied down to what you want, because you might actually find that you didn't want some of those things after all.

***Wants can blind you to needs.***

Ah yes, 'needs'.

We've been here before.

Men don't have needs, right?

I'm pretty sure if that were true, we'd all be plants. Even plants need connection though. And I don't know about you, but I wasn't designed to just sit in some dirt and grow every now and again. (Plants can be pretty, just so you don't think I have some super weird vendetta against vegetation.)

The unfortunate truth is that it's so easy to paper over our needs in our relationships in exchange for what we want. We think that if we put that square peg in that round hole, everything will be okay. But it simply does not equate. As such, our **needs** often get swept under the rug for a sense of false comfort that doesn't actually fix anything.

Your needs are so important and they far outweigh your wants. But sadly, our ability to ignore our needs creates unnecessary tension in our relationships and can cause us to miss the boat completely, passing up what could have been a great opportunity all because it didn't look like what we thought we wanted.

The beautiful part of this process is that often we won't even realise the things we need from someone else in a relationship without first taking the risk to trust them with our heart. Sometimes you just need to be willing to press 'go' to see where the road will lead. But 'go' can seem incredibly daunting. I've spent a good portion of my life waiting to see if the magical 'green light' from Jesus on relationships appears like a giant flashing neon sign from the sky. As it turns out, that idea can detract from your happiness, because you might miss something great whilst you sit there waiting for the starting flag to be raised.

I'm not saying you should pursue something that clearly isn't good for you, but it can be so easy to spend a long time waiting for what you think is the right thing, which is often based upon cultural ideas, which in all honesty is a warped reality of what you'll find when you fall in love.

***Love is a choice.*** And yet love is also a feeling. The way you love someone, and how much you're willing to trust them with, is defined by the choices you make with that person. The more you grow and trust someone, the easier it is to trust them with your heart. Ironically it can also make trusting them with your heart that much more daunting, as it is probably the most intimate thing a person can do. It is the height of vulnerability. You won't be trusting with someone, and your heart won't be safe, if your choices are based out of fear when trying to connect with someone.

If you try to build a relationship on a foundation of fear and mistrust you'll find very quickly that the cracks won't just be in the foundations, but all over the place.

*The first step to trusting someone can be the most intimidating.*

I know what it is like to feel as though your heart is out there on a tightrope, with no guarantee of being caught if you fall. That's why trust is so important and it can't be fabricated. Trust in relationships comes from a place of security. If you don't feel safe and secure with someone, then it's highly likely you won't trust them.

Maybe you're now sitting there wondering what it is I actually mean by the term 'needs'. Well, let me try and break it down for you.

As a guy, I've had the idea sold to me that what I want in a woman is the blonde or brunette supermodel with the flawless figure (whatever that means). My supposed desires are heavily influenced by how sexualised the media is. And I know that women have had the same images of men painted in their minds — (let's all take a moment to celebrate our 'flawless figures'). In essence, this idealism is actually killing love and relationships.

I know how influenced I am by what I see, what I place my attention in and what I'm told. *Just imagine the power the media could have if it presented positive imagery of how to view people, and not objectify them.*

**Sex sells.** You're far more likely to grab someone's attention with a half naked human on a magazine cover because humans are naturally sexual beings. Your eyes are drawn to it because that's how your body works. I'm not really preaching anything new here. ***But think for a second about how drastically this is warping your relationships.*** If you're trained (by what you've been exposed to) to look for certain things in someone you find attractive, then real people will always fall short. They aren't what you *want.*

Think about how many people have passed up wonderful opportunities for happy romantic relationships due to thinking they're looking for something entirely different. Until you take off your rose—tinted lenses, you won't truly appreciate someone for the beautiful human they are.

And that's where the wonder of finding out what you need comes into play. The person who fulfils your needs and desires may be right in front of you, but you're looking in the wrong place.

What I *need* is someone to make me feel loved, affirmed and cherished. I *need* someone to make me feel safe when I process the things that scare me, and when my vulnerability is in full flow. I *need* someone that brings everything in my life back to Jesus, to remind me that He has it all in His hands. I *need* someone who I can grow with, and have fun with. I *need* someone who loves me for the oddball that I can be, and actually finds my weirdness endearing.

*Notice how this has nothing to do with image.* Image is merely face value. It doesn't show what's inside the person. Sacrificing your supposed idea of what you think you want in someone allows you to see someone for who they really are. It removes the false sense of security that an 'image—first' culture presents. When you choose to love someone based upon who they are, you then choose to dismiss the detrimental idea of false attractiveness that's based purely upon looks. And you might also find them more attractive. Looks fade over time, but a person's character will stay with them forever. ***Make the choice to fall for who someone is, not what they look like.*** It'll benefit you for the rest of your life.

# LOVE IS A CHOICE

I decided to split this chapter up a little bit, as there's so much to unpack, but mainly I wanted to focus on that statement right there, "love is a choice".

In a society full of buzzwords, that one phrase can be thrown around at will, and often not given much attention. Attention is exactly what it needs, though.

Previously, I talked about the romantic notion of falling in love that Hollywood has done so well to feed us, and I think acknowledgement of that is great but it doesn't necessarily tell us how to combat the fake romance beast.

By setting unobtainable relationship goals it's almost as if the real script for how to successfully navigate a loving relationship has been accidentally swept into the bin.

I'm the first to admit that I don't have it figured out, but what I do know is that the discussion needs to be had. I cannot stress enough how important communication is in a healthy and loving relationship. Good communication alleviates tension, and doesn't leave anyone second guessing what's actually going on. It takes away the ability to misinterpret. Honesty has set the bar.

*In any form of relationship, connection should be the goal.*

If I'm not connecting with the person I'm spending time with, then I'm wasting my time. With this in mind, **connection and love are a part of the same family.**

If you truly care about someone, then you will want to connect with them, hear their heart and be there for them when they need you. When I end up having a disagreement with someone I care about, my goal is always to stay connected with them. And sometimes that can mean fighting through the pain that might be caused by disagreement, because I know that on the other side of that pain is a greater level of connection.

When you decide to stay connected with someone, you're choosing to love them in that moment. The choice to love someone is much more powerful when it's hard to do. Those choices will define how that relationship plays out. They'll set the solid foundations that the relationship needs, and will also set the benchmark for how to handle conflict in the future.

Most of us are wired to react and not respond when it comes to conflict. It's just human nature. And if you don't think you're an emotional person, you might just be suppressing those emotions and feelings. We're all designed to feel, whether you want to engage with the emotions or not. If you choose to **respond** rather than react, then you can reprogram the lens through which you view pain, conflict and disagreement.

*Where reaction screams in retaliation to pain, response says "I'm going to hear you without interrupting and yelling back when I feel hurt, because that will only cause disconnection."*

Responding doesn't mean you have to agree on every point. You're allowed to disagree with the other person, but you are responsible for how you react to what they share. Just as they are not responsible for your emotions, you are also not responsible for their reaction.

I believe it's entirely possible to have a constructive conversation that deals with and addresses the pain caused by another person, and resolve the situation without inflaming it further. As long as your aim is to stay connected (and value the other person more than what they may have said or done) then conflict should never be something that terrifies you.

If you choose to respond well to conflict, it communicates that you value the other person in the situation. That choice also shows that you value yourself highly, and won't be drawn into unnecessary conflict.

**Choosing to love someone isn't always a simple decision, but it can be the most rewarding one you ever make.**

# 'THE GAME'

You don't need to be particularly switched on to see that we are currently in a society full of messages that, in their very nature, seem to be anti—commitment. 'Hook—up' culture is prevalent everywhere you look. From Tinder, to accidental 'snaps' that end up giving away far more than should ever be given to someone so freely.

*And to be honest, it breaks my heart.*

But that's the culture in which we live. We want everything now, and if we can't have everything now then we sure as hell want an explanation and validation as to *why we can't have it now.* Everything is readily accessible, and that also includes human beings.

The idea of 'no strings attached' is one that is highly appealing to much of society, since it doesn't involve a whole lot of emotional sacrifice. (Oh I went there.) What it presents is a quick and immediate connection with someone that fulfils certain needs we all have. But what it often fails to address is the other deeper connections that can be made through this same process, and it tends to gloss over the longing we all have to feel known fully by someone else.

The number of people aged 16 and over in England and Wales who are married has dropped by almost 5% from 54.8% to 50.6%, the lowest since 2002.1 People are now seeking cohabitation as an alternative to marriage,2 meaning that the idea of lifelong commitment is an ideal that seems to be fading more and more into obscurity. It's sad. And it's becoming a game. When your relationships become a game, they lessen the value of the people involved in these relationships, giving nobody a chance at creating stability for their romance.

If we're constantly placing our gaze somewhere other than the one to which we're committed, what does that say about our relationships? Are we even committed in the first place if we can't keep our focus on the ones we've chosen to be with?

This belief that there is always something or someone better out there is destroying what could be incredibly happy and health relationships. It gets people into the mindset that they will never have what they want or need with the one they're currently with. If we look at the dating world through that lens, we're always going to be on the look out for something that seems more appealing — a 'newer, more attractive' model or version of what we currently have. A sense of Materialism has crept into relationships in an alarming way.

For many reasons, I don't like this idea of "The Game". If you're willing to play The Game, and play the field at the cost of someone else, then you're certainly not ready to get into a loving, committed relationship.

*That may seem harsh, but it's true.*

***What we feed on is ultimately what we replicate.***

This generation has been exposed to the idea that relationships are both flexible and temporary. We love the ability to be malleable, and change, pick up or drop things at the first sign of things getting scary. And by scary, I don't mean things that genuinely terrify people. I mean the things that we run away from because we're too terrified to confront them; our fears.

***Our fear of committment. Our fear of being hurt. Our independence. Our fear of letting someone into the deepest, darkest parts of us, and believing that someone could actually love those parts.***

You see, in reality the game is something that is

designed to keep us from dealing with our pain. By placing multiple 'options' in front of us and by keeping us in the mindset that anything we find here is fleeting, we open up to the idea of the game. In actuality, if we're constantly on the look out for a 'quick fix' on the relationship front, then the likelihood is that we're not actually dealing with important things going on inside of us.

If you find yourself jumping from one girl (or guy) to another, ask yourself why. Are you happy in a cycle of temporary acceptance and premature affection, or are you really avoiding something that's going on inside of you?

*We're a generation that's crying out for true love.*

We want to be known, loved and appreciated for who we are. But is that possible in a society that says a temporary fix is better than a real solution? Talk about putting a band aid on a bullet wound.

It distresses me because I see it unfolding before my eyes on an almost daily basis. We're becoming a society that's far more comfortable with compromise than completion. If we're really seeking someone with whom we can share the ecstatic highs and incomparable lows, then we need to start building a foundation of trust with one another. And I find it difficult to see how that's possible when we're playing the relationship game. If we get bored when things don't go our way with that girl, it's a problem. If all we're looking for is someone who fits into the Victoria's Secret model image, it's a problem.

We're compromising on image, and in turn allowing that to define how we see the opposite sex. Our expectations are impossible to ever meet as they are set so far out of this world and reality. And because they go unmet we start looking for things that will numb that disappointment and pain that we carry. We've come to believe that silencing the voice of pain is easier than confronting it and moving towards wholeness.

'The game' is killing relationships as they've been traditionally defined. It sets people up with the idea that there's *always* something or someone better out there for you, and when you lock yourself into that mindset you can quite easily miss out on the beauty that God has placed directly in front of you. What is this way of thinking doing for people's self image? I shudder to think. If we're feeding each other the spiel that you have to look a certain way to attract someone who will make you feel loved, then that's one message. But if we're also telling them that they could be dropped just like *that* because there's someone else who's caught our eye? How on earth can we expect anyone to feel beautiful in their own skin if we've created a culture that's constantly on the lookout for something better?

*Comparison is a killer, and it has crept into far too many relationships.*

***This culture of passing people around like hot coals because they fill a need for a moment is destroying our capacity to comprehend the wonder of real commitment. And if you're constantly on the look out for someone who fits the bill of your fantasies, you're likely to miss the person of your dreams.***

I heard it said a few years ago "hurt people hurt people" and recently I've been able to witness what that actually looks like. If you find yourself hopping from one relationship to another without time to breathe, it's likely that you might want to take a look inside and see how your heart is doing.

As humans we tend to take the route that keeps us the furthest away from danger. We avoid the things that present us with the possibility of pain. However, if you're already hurting then you might not see how your actions are affecting those around you. You might think you're completely fine and you wonder why every girl or guy you meet seems to do something wrong and can't quite keep you happy. Here's a newsflash: if you're continually shutting down potential relationships because they're just "not quite *it*" **the problem might not be them**; The real obstacle might just be you.

I'm not attempting to throw blame on anyone here. What I'm trying to do is get people to realise that lack of commitment is becoming a real problem in the dating world.

If we continue down this road it is possible that long—term relationships will become extinct.

I have a lot of passion in this area because I want to see everyone live in relationship to the best of their ability, and anything contradictory means we're not fully appreciating what Jesus did for us. He died to restore connection between us and the Father by covering our iniquities with His blood.

The fullness of Christ is personified through love—fuelled connection. That's my mantra whenever I feel myself or my significant other steering towards disconnect. Jesus died so that we may experience *fullness* in every area of our lives, and in relationship with one another in this, we are *always* fighting for connection with each other.

What I want is to see people who are so filled with a passionate pursuit of one another (because we know the value in that connection) that the idea of giving up on someone doesn't even cross our minds.

*People are worth pursuing.*

Jesus set the model for that on the cross. Shouldn't we be following that with all that we are?

# SEX

How many of you just skipped to this chapter because this word immediately got your attention? *Thought so. I know I would have.* To be perfectly honest, when I started writing this book all those pages ago, I didn't think I was going to tackle this topic. But somewhere along the journey, Jesus told me to share what I've learned.

*So here we are.*

Sex, unfortunately, has become synonymous with pornography in today's culture *(It pained me to even write that sentence.)*

The reality is that sex *does* indeed sell. It's probably the thing that catches people's attention the most. It's nearly impossible to walk down a high street now, wherever you may be, and not find your eyes drawn to a half—naked human adorning the window display of certain shops. But it's not just window displays that catch our attention.

We're a generation that have become known as 'scrollers'. And I cannot recall the amount of times I have been scrolling through Instagram or Twitter and suddenly see something in my feed that causes me to either stop or speed up my scrolling. My ability to stop or keep scrolling is dictated by how strong I feel that day (to be perfectly honest). What I feed myself becomes my expectation, and I'd much rather feed myself reality and truth than fantasy.

*Sex is accessible to anyone and everyone.*

The fact that sex is so readily available is what makes the challenges we all face that much harder. After all, if we can have access to immediate (but often false) pleasure and satisfaction, then why would we place value on something like sex? And thus the pornography industry was born, and flourished.

**I can't say this strongly enough: *I detest pornography.***

I say that as someone who has had far too many years of their own life taken by this destructive drug. To me, there is absolutely nothing positive whatsoever to its existence. It is designed to destroy something that God created for our pleasure. *It warps everything.* It warps our view of the other sex, our ability to comprehend intimacy, our stability and our ability to relate to one another. It's easily as damaging as other hardcore drugs, but it affects different areas of our lives. It destroys relationships and marriages. Porn takes away our ability to understand true happiness in relation to the opposite sex. It ruins our expectations of what sex and consensual relationships look like, because everything about it is fantasy.

It's also a silent killer, because there is such a level of shame attached to it that it becomes far easier to not talk about. It's the elephant in the corner of the room that everyone knows is there, but it's never addressed. (I'll mention here that I think the church has done a terrible job at talking about this subject and removing shame from it, but I'll get into that in a little bit...)

Ugh, I just ***hate*** it.

I remember vividly the first time I was exposed to it. I was sitting in my friend's bedroom and we decided to play Russian Roulette with websites. But in actuality, we knew exactly what we were doing. The real question was whether we could see what we wanted to see, and then shut it down quick enough before a parent walked into the room.

I look back on that instance and grieve the years that the devil took from me. The pathways in my brain that had to be rewritten and washed out. The understanding of the true beauty of women that I wish had been instilled in me in that instance, instead of some bastardised, objectified image of what sexual attraction to a woman looks like.

The devil is a thief. He will seek to steal, kill and destroy whatever he can get his hands on. And for so many of us, that area of greatest weakness is surrounding our sex drive and desire for true intimacy.

*I write this today as someone who is walking in the freedom afforded me by Jesus. That is not to say that there aren't daily struggles, and I have to make choices in every passing moment as to what I believe to be true and righteous. But I do know there's a greater level of intimacy that we can walk in as humans, and it doesn't need to be tied to unrealistic expectations and fantasies regarding the opposite sex.*

I mentioned briefly before that I think the global church has done an incredibly substandard job of presenting the beauty and priceless nature of sexuality and purity. We've been fed ideas over the years that have caused us to run from truth because of fear of condemnation, when actually we *should* be running towards our convictions.

A few years ago, I felt Jesus calling me to spend some time in northern California at a church called Bethel. I ended up spending three wonderful years there with friends I shall cherish for the rest of my life, but more—so the lessons I learned while I was there are ones that will stick with me and define me for the rest of my life.

I remember the first service I walked into at Bethel Church, where a man named Kris Vallotton was speaking about a 'Moral Revolution'. His message was a redefining of how we view sex, and how it is possible to remove the stigma attached to the topic. For the first time in my life I felt like someone was finally tackling taboo topics in church.

I grew up going to church, but there were certain topics that were never really addressed. They were too controversial. But Jesus never shied away from controversy, so why should we?

To hear the topic of sex talked about so freely and openly allowed me to see that this is an area God has ordained as a vital part to our healthy human existence within the correct confines of covenant relationship with your husband or wife. For years I felt like it was impossible to bring this subject up because of the shame attached to it. I couldn't bring up the topic of sex in church, so how on earth could I possibly bring up the issue I had with porn?

And this is precisely the problem I want to abolish.

As Christians, we've created this culture where we talk about the things Jesus did, and the way God loves us, which is great, and obviously I agree with this. But when it comes to tackling things that might be seen as controversial, we tend to shy away. After all, shame isn't something that we want to befriend. And if we have, then we certainly don't want others knowing about our inner most, darkest secrets.

*But that's the problem right there.* Secrets are removed from the light, and light is a purifying agent. Jesus desires a level of relationship with us where we can bring *anything and everything* to Him, without fear. We should actually be marching headfirst into controversy and discomfort, because we're backed up by the best coach of all time.

I honestly can't recall more than a few times where the topic of pornography was broached in church when I was growing up. I remember the altar calls at (Christian summer festival) Soul Survivor for anyone wanting freedom from addiction. I stood up at least three times over the years, but it honestly didn't feel like much changed. What I actually needed was to run to Jesus with this problem. He wanted to replace my shame with security and purity.

For so many years I kept this battle in the shadows, terrified of what someone might think if I told them I was struggling in this area. In reality though an honest conversation was exactly what I needed.

When you bring a problem out of the darkness and into the light, the power of the darkness is exposed as falsehood. Light drives out darkness wherever it is allowed to shine.

So here I am, multiple years into my own freedom. And my intention is to **never** let that back into my life. My values have been realigned with what Jesus says about me, and about women. The choices I make now are rooted in a belief that the fight is worth it.

***I'm here to tell you that no battle is too great for Jesus to overcome. Nothing is so bad that it can't be restored.***

Porn warped my view of women. This led to the destruction of the beauty that surrounds sex. When you consume images of women in either barely—there clothing (or none whatsoever) you lose track of the person's value. That's what happens when you're only thinking "what can I get out of this situation?"

What I thought I wanted from a significant other was someone who had big *this*, big *that*, nothing *there*, and wasn't scared to do anything. How many other people are living out of that same mindset? It is so damaging, and it's destroying so many lives because there is no element of reality attached to it. The only reality is that it causes more harm than good.

Porn was so destructive to my view of women that it took a complete shift in my thinking (by Jesus) to understand that women are there to be adored, cherished and valued as daughters of the King. In a society that overtly sexualises everything, we constantly run the risk of devaluing both men and women on a minute by minute basis. Reality is not reflected by what you experience through a 13—inch computer screen.

The sad likelihood is that anyone involved in the industry of pornography has lost an aspect of their own self—worth. Or maybe they never knew their own worth in the first place. When you ask God to view these men and women as He sees them, it's amazing how your perspective shifts. I had to start looking at it from the perspective of "that's somebody's son or daughter: would I want that for my own kids?" Of course I wouldn't. It's heartbreaking to imagine something like that, and it only drives me to show more love. Has anyone ever told porn actors that they were unconditionally loved? I'm afraid the answer is likely "no".

Porn has done such a magnificent job of removing the wonder and beauty from sex, and making it a commodity that can be sold and devalued through a click here or a swipe there. Sex is something that God created for our own pleasure.

But what I have realised over the last year or so is that each of us can protect the wonder and beauty of sex. We can protect it with the choices we make on a daily basis. The choices I make today will affect how much is left to be discovered at the right time and in the right place, and this is where porn and Jesus are at loggerheads. Porn teaches that you can have everything right now, that everything is easily accessible. But by preserving the beauty of sex for the confines of a committed, loving marriage, you see the reward of waiting. God wants to preserve the wonders of sex for a certain point in your relationship with your significant other, because it's that important.

*Porn says "why wait?"*
*Jesus says "she/he is worth the wait."*

Now, this is not to say that the fight to save sexual intimacy for marriage gets easier when you get into a relationship — I thought it would with someone else fighting for it with me. Actually it gets more difficult. Now finding myself in a loving, committed relationship, the temptation is stronger than ever before to compromise our values and experience that ultimate level of intimacy and connection. But I am fortunate enough to have someone who values the fight for that intimate finish line as highly as I do. We know that we are building something far greater than a moment's experience. A healthy future together is far more important to both of us than a compromise here and there.

The problem we have as a society is that we're seeking constant affection and acknowledgement. We no longer understand the concept of 'wait'. It's a hard sell at the best of times, and much harder when you're talking to teenagers who don't want to be told how to live their lives.

As a teenage boy I was presented with images that were designed to be shared in the confines of a marriage. For many boys, it's difficult to shut things out of your brain when you're so visually stimulated. And that's the challenge — we've got a generation of young people who are pretty much numbed to things that previous generations thought were inappropriate. You see it in newspaper headlines, on TV, and it's reflected in the choices that we make when we're on our own with nobody else looking.

Sustaining innocence is an uphill battle when you're exposed to so much at such a young age. Privacy is something that people don't respect much anymore. Look at what happened in 2014, when private and intimate photos of celebrities were leaked onto the internet. Society knows that sex sells, and it sells big. If you can get the latest scandalous scoop, you get it by **whatever means necessary.**

*The things that we guard highly are often those things that carry the most value. And people will pay anything to claim something valuable.*

The part that breaks my heart is that I've learned a lot of this in reverse. I've had to go through trials, make daily choices about what I actually value and what I want my future to look like. But how many years were wasted looking for fulfilment somewhere that always left me coming up empty? Too many is the answer.

More than half of my life has been spent fighting the invisible foe that goes after my purity on a daily, minute—by—minute basis, but it wasn't until Jesus realigned my value system, that I was truly able to change direction.

The reason this breaks my heart is because I look now at the generation below me, and wonder how many of them have spent years battling the same thing? How many of them are still trapped in this cycle that tells them that there is no way out, and that they're destined to live this pattern for the rest of their days?

By teaching our kids to value men and women like God values them, then suddenly the negative narrative becomes a lot quieter. What would it look like if we could change the narrative our kids see in front of them? Instead of sexualising so many men and women because that's what 'society tells us to do', maybe we should rewrite the story. There are many families out there facing this battle, and by choosing to fight it they are setting the foundations for future generations to build upon.

The battle isn't an easy one. We all know that. But the model Jesus lays out is the one I want to follow. In one of my favourite parables which describes Jesus as the great Shepherd, Jesus leaves the ninety-nine sheep to rescue the one that had run off. It shows how much love He has for every individual in the Kingdom of God. But more than that, it presents us with another *narrative.*

What if we were the generation that embraced our identity as the "one" that was rescued? And what if that meant that we in turn ended up changing the lives of the other ninety-nine? How do we do that?

Here's a good place to start. *Value sex for what it is*— a beautiful expression of love designed for covenant.

For those who are reading this and are still battling that disease of pornography (because that's what it is, and diseases can be cured), I release my own breakthrough over you. I pray that Jesus would loosen the chains in your mind, and lead you in the steps you need to take to take back what the enemy has stolen.

*Don't lose hope.*

***Remember that the Victor is on your side.***

# THE JOY OF GIVING UP

*"Crying is only going make it worse"*

I've heard it said so many times that crying is just a form of weakness. That if you end up crying, you're 'not a man'. This sentiment goes beyond personal experience; it is a cultural understanding and an expectation of machoism.

If you cry, you're seen as vulnerable. And depending on your interpretation of that word, that can either be a good thing or a bad thing. To me, vulnerability is a beautiful thing because it shows me that I am in touch with what's truly going on inside of me in that moment. However, to someone else who may have been taught differently, and the connotation changes dramatically.

I like to look at it this way: tears are essentially a release of pent up energy, emotion and frustration. If you don't let them out, you're basically a ticking time bomb that could explode at any point, and you could explode in a variety of ways — many of them dangerous. Where do you think anger, bad temperament and violence stem from? It's very likely that individuals who respond aggressively to the world around them do so because they are neglecting what it going on inside of them. And they do that because they've been told by someone, somewhere that if you are emotional, you are weak. And men must be seen as strong. *Crying makes it better though.*

Tears are a form of release. All of that pent up anxiety, anger, stress, nervousness — it can simply be dealt with by letting those emotions out in a healthy (and natural) way. This is a lesson that I have learned over the past couple of years, although it wasn't easy. Somewhere along the way I decided to start believing in a false sense of masculinity which included 'ignoring my emotions'.

**Here's a disclaimer: Don't do it. It's not worth it.**

*(Best read in an Essex accent. And if you're not sure what that is, open up YouTube and type in The Only Way is Essex — You're welcome.)*

At some point, I decided to close myself off to my own emotions and put a stop to the most natural form of dealing with how I was feeling — crying. I had suddenly agreed in my head with the ridiculous notion that crying is a form of weakness, and that people I shouldn't let see me cry because then what will they think of me? I can't be seen as weak. For starters, I'm six foot five. I need that respect from people. I can't be seen as a wimp.

*Oh, how gloriously naive I was.*

Fast forward a couple of years and there I was, sitting in my bedroom and feeling like my insides were about to explode with sheer frustration. Everything had built up over the years, and even though I scratched the surface of dealing with things emotionally, I never really got to the root of what was going on. As I sat there slowly swaying from side to side, it suddenly dawned on me:

*We were not designed to live life like a carbonated drink in a bottle that's been shaken to the point that the cap is about to blow through a window.* Holding everything in just wasn't working for me anymore. Not that it ever actually worked for me in the first place. And how I wish I could tell you that it was a pretty sight.

*It wasn't.*

But the beauty in that experience is that the Potter can remake and remould the clay to how it should be and, perhaps, how it was meant to be all along.

So there I was, a blubbering, exhausted snotty mess on my bed at 3am. I had finally given up. I had done remarkably well in holding on to my frustrations and my pain, and shoving them deep, deep down inside of me so that they never really saw the light of day again, until this moment.

As I sat crying I realised this was not how I was supposed to live my life. I was certainly not experiencing the fullness that Jesus talked about with such vigour in the Scriptures. In this perfect moment of sublime irony, I had actually discovered what it looked like to be a real man.

The cultural challenge we currently face is the expectation to throw all of these walls up to 'protect ourselves', but these walls are made of drywall, not concrete. This expectation is only making us more fragile as people, and as men of God.

What happened that cold winter evening was something that shaped the way I now approach every area of my life. I decided to give up and let Jesus deal with whatever it was that He wanted to deal with inside of me. For me, in that moment, it meant dealing with the lie that I was never going to find happiness in relationship and that I would never find a wife.

It took me getting to that breaking point in order for Him to show me that all He wants from His kids is to run to Him when we have problems that we can't solve. I surrendered, completely. It might sound cliché, but it's absolutely true. And let me tell you, *giving up was the most liberating experience of my life.*

It allowed me to step into the freedom of not feeling pressure internally and externally in every decision that I make. It showed me that what many can perceive as weakness is actually a sign of great strength. Vulnerability is a beautiful thing, and it's so important to living a healthy life.

*I've learnt that in order to have true power and control over your life, you actually need to give up.*

**Give it all up.**

**Become a mess when you need to be a mess. Feel what it is you need to feel. Don't shut it all away, because that just creates a false sense of power and you begin to think that you're fine when you're really not.**

You see, crying is not weakness. It is necessary so that you can be healthy. I think the reason so many see it as a form of weakness is because it's the most vulnerable expression you can make as a human. It happens when you have nothing left. So naturally, if you're afraid of vulnerability, you certainly won't want to embrace tears.

Do yourself a favour — don't listen to what society tells you about 'being a man'. Instead, choose to listen to what's going on inside of you. You'll be amazed at the difference it'll make to your life.

# about the author

Ed is a writer, musician, creative and author of his first published work, Feelings Are Stupid. He has spent the past few years creating music and written content with independent record label Orphan No More, based in Bath, UK. Ed can often be found reminiscing about the nostalgic 90s, pulling his hair out watching Manchester United and drinking a good cup of coffee.

*Ed and his wife Janey currently reside in Preston, UK.*

www.ingramcontent.com/pod-product-compliance
Lightning Source LLC
Chambersburg PA
CBHW051026030426
42336CB00015B/2738
* 9 7 8 1 7 3 2 1 9 6 4 6 9 *